HOW TO DEAL WITH AUTISTIC CHILDREN:

A parental guide to understanding and managing kids with autism

Ronny A. Graham

Table of contents:

Chapter 1
Chapter 2
Chapter 3
Chapter 4
Chapter 5
Chapter 6
Chapter 7

Chapter 1

What it's really like for a child with autism:

What is a mental imbalance range jumble?

It is continuously difficult and depleting to Parent a small kid. At the point when you are the parent of a kid with a chemical imbalance, the difficulties increase. It very well may be challenging for yourself as well as your youngster to bond. Your kid with mental imbalance loves you, although they may not show it in the standard ways. You might need to track down various ways of associating. Zeroing in on the affection you offer can make this and other troublesome assignments feasible.

Youngsters with mental imbalance vary from most others in more than one way, including:

How they impart with others

How they interface with others

The manners in which they learn

How they act

One more name for chemical imbalance is chemical imbalance range jumble (ASD). This term mirrors the variety of individuals with a chemical imbalance. How much assistance they expect to work can fluctuate broadly.

At the point when you are the parent of a kid with a mental imbalance, the difficulties increase. Being a parent of a medically introverted kid might make you feel culpability, misery, tension, disappointment, and outrage.

How is ASD analyzed?

To analyze chemical imbalance, well-being experts search for two primary indications of ASD. To start with, the kid will miss the mark on relational abilities and interactive abilities that most youngsters have at a similar age. Second, the kid will show an example of conduct that incorporates:

Activities that are rehashed again and again
Customs
An emphasis on small subtleties
In youngsters with ASD, these characteristics are available to some extent that influences their capability.

Normally, kids with mental imbalances likewise have tactile issues. They might be delicate to lights, sounds, scents, and surfaces, or they might look for extraordinary tactile excitement. Their capacity to think and to talk can fluctuate generally.

Here and their individuals accept that their kids can't have chemical imbalance since they are profoundly verbal. While certain youngsters with ASD are non-verbal, others are very garrulous.

They have a great deal to say regarding the subjects that interest them yet don't see how to carry on discussions.

Tolerating your youngster's analysis
If your kid gets conclusion of mental imbalance, you will likely experience a surge of feelings, including:

Culpability. You might feel answerable for your kid's problem, even though information about what causes mental imbalance is nowhere near total.
Despondency:
You might feel a feeling of misfortune because your kid won't have the existence you believed them should have. Additionally, the existence you imagined for yourself should change.
Uneasiness. You are probably going to stress over your kid's future. What will befall your kid assuming you bite the dust or can never again focus on them?

Disappointment. Loved ones might disappoint you with an absence of understanding. In broad daylight, others might think your kid gets out of hand, which is disturbing.

Outrage. You might end up being angry at the absence of help you get from your companion or accomplice, relatives, and companions. You may not get the assistance you are anticipating from social administrations.

Optimistically, it may very well be a help to have a name for your youngster's side effects. You will likewise discover that there are medicines, even though there is no solution for mental imbalance. Those with ASD can develop and advance. A conclusion empowers you to begin that cycle.

Get your loved ones in the group
You will require help and backing. That implies offering your kid's analysis to other people. Be ready for protection

from the finding. Many individuals have assumptions about kids with a chemical imbalance. Your youngster may not fit the photos to them. Family members might require time to handle this data before they can acknowledge it.

You can assist those near you with understanding mental imbalance by guiding them to great wellsprings of data. Requesting that companions or family members go on medical services visits with you can build their comprehension. In any case, almost certainly, certain individuals will track down deception and offer it to you. Do whatever it takes not to go overboard. Recollect that they're attempting to help.

Figure out how to associate with your kid Having a youngster with a chemical imbalance here and there means learning better approaches to the interface. Since youngsters with mental imbalances fluctuate so a lot, your kid might not have a portion of these issues. However, numerous kids with chemical imbalance have these qualities:

They may not figure out looks and other non-verbal correspondences.
They dislike being contacted and be awkward with actual articulations of friendship.
They take things in a real sense and experience difficulty with humor, expressions, and metaphors.
They might be seriously keen on a certain something and not be able to discuss anything more.
They can need affability and may express terrible things.
Assuming that you're patient and stay positive, you'll track down ways of associating with your mentally unbalanced kid.

Get it done bat for your youngster

If you're the parent of a youngster with a chemical imbalance, you'll likely need to advocate for your kid. That implies going to bat for your youngster, as a rule, incorporating at home and openly. You might feel more great assuming you imagine yourself standing for all kids with a chemical imbalance.

One more part of supporting includes knowing your youngster's privileges and pushing for them to get administration, particularly from your educational system. While going to gatherings about your kid, make certain to:

Keep great records
Make a hard copy of everything
Take somebody with you to tune in and offer help
Be self-assured yet remain mentally collected

You can likewise advocate for chemical imbalance at the nearby, state, and public levels. Join associations that will let you know how to function for further developed care. You can give a discourse, compose a letter, go to a convention, or participate in alternate ways.

Keep up with other significant connections

Having a youngster with mental imbalance influences day-to-day life. In one study, moms of youngsters with mental imbalances said their relationships have endured. A few said they felt genuinely far off from their mates. They additionally said they needed more time for their different youngsters. A portion of different youngsters said that they felt ignored.

Feelings of anxiety go up when a family incorporates a youngster with mental imbalance. Although there are no simple arrangements, it might serve to:

Ask your medical services group for help and exhortation
Invest one-on-one energy with every youngster
Search for a care group for kin of youngsters with a chemical imbalance
Go along with at least one care group for guardians

Focusing on a youngster with a mental imbalance can influence your procuring power. You could need to surrender your work or change to a lower-paying position with better hours. In certain families, guardians take on additional responsibilities to get more cash flow, yet this implies additional time away from home.

Chapter 2

The emotions of a child with autism:

The Test
TIP: It Will Pass
TIP: Oversee Implosions
TIP: Learn While Quiet
TIP: Take It Off

It's a fantasy that kids with mental imbalance do not have many or no feelings. Nothing could be further from reality. Kids with chemical imbalances might become close to home for various reasons or unexpectedly express their feelings, however, they have similar however many sentiments as anybody else.[1]

Now and again, jokes around mental imbalance might be considered close to home than a portion of their run-of-the-mill peers.[2] They can experience difficulty letting their sentiments out, however, and may require help communicating them.

Why Feelings Are Testing
Advanced chemical imbalance can be very challenging. From one perspective, you have the language and mental abilities to be set in a common climate. Then again, you miss the mark on friendly, correspondence, and chief working abilities to work well when a change occurs.3

Simultaneously, you might be adapting to tactile brokenness, uneasiness, or different issues that make splendid lights, clear commotions, and elevated standards remarkably difficult to manage.4

At the point when jokes around with mental imbalance, even advanced kids, become very baffled or irate, and they frequently carry on. At the point when they do, they might act in a manner that amaze or shocks individuals around them. For instance, they may:

Complete implosion like a lot more youthful youngster, with tears and yelling
Take off from a tough spot, once in a while jeopardizing themselves
Become forceful or self-oppressive
Blow up to the circumstance and not be able to self-quiet
Not being able to deal with coherent data that, in another circumstance, would assist them with quieting down
End up being too upset to even consider paying attention to quieting ideas
Display self-stimulatory ways of behaving (hand fluttering, and so on.)
Many, while possibly not most, kids who are analyzed on the mental imbalance range experience issues controlling their feelings and keeping a quiet state.1 They may likewise be adapting to a portion of

the constraints they feel yet can't express or grasp in alternate ways.

In some cases "gentle" chemical imbalance is everything except. It tends to be very difficult, particularly for youngsters and their folks. Nobody needs to see their youngster in torment when something isn't working out.

The Inclination Will Pass
Remind your youngster (and yourself) that crying is brought about by an inclination and that feeling will pass like a foreboding shadow. The sun will come out again even though it seems like the sky is falling.

Assist your kid with figuring out how to take a couple of slow full breaths when they initially start to feel upset. Practice this routinely when they're not disturbed. Do it with them. Tell them that we all, youngsters and grown-ups, lash out and need to figure out how to quiet ourselves.

Implosions

A few implosions might include your kid's responses and their need to figure out how to manage responsive qualities and disappointments and regulate themselves; to track down solace and consolation from the inside.

You can assist your kid with figuring out how to manage outrageous close-to-home responses by giving them ways of quieting or soothing themselves before going on. There are numerous ways of doing this and the vast majority of us track down our specific manners over the long haul.

For instance, it assists a few kids with being separated from everyone else for a couple of seconds. It helps other people to sit and converse with somebody or to redirect their considerations a tad.

Get the hang of During Quiet Times

In unbiased times, when your kid isn't vexed, you can converse with them about ways of holding their feelings back from erupting. By figuring out how to possess their nervousness and dissatisfaction, they can overcome it with just enough persistence or by making things in more modest strides.

You can work with your kid and their instructors in regards to the most ideal ways for them to figure out how to quiet down.

Take It Off

During times that you realize a complete implosion is reasonable, you can once in a while remove it by consulting with your kid about it ahead of time and examining how they could keep away from it this time. You could try and need to offer compensation for doing as such.

Chapter 3

How to understand and support your child:

Everything you can manage is to begin treatment immediately. Look for help when you suspect something's off-base. Try not to stand by to check whether your youngster will look up some other time or grow out of the issue. Don't for even a moment hang tight for an authority conclusion. The prior youngsters with chemical imbalance range jumble find support, the more prominent their opportunity of treatment achievement. Early intercession is the best method for accelerating your kid's turn of events and diminishing the side effects of mental imbalance over life expectancy.

Find out about mental imbalance. The more you are familiar with mental imbalance range jumble, the better prepared you'll be to settle on informed choices for your kid. Teach yourself about the treatment choices, seek clarification on some pressing issues, and partake in all treatment choices.

Turn into a specialist for your youngster. Sort out the thing that triggers your child's difficult or troublesome ways of behaving and what gets a positive reaction. What does your youngster view as distressing or alarming? Quieting? Awkward? Agreeable? Assuming you comprehend what influences your kid, you'll be better at investigating issues and forestalling or changing circumstances that cause trouble.

Acknowledge your youngster, peculiarities or not. As opposed to zeroing in on how your mentally unbalanced youngster is unique concerning different kids and what the person is "missing," practice acknowledgment. Partake in your child's unique characteristics, celebrate little victories, and quit contrasting your kid with others. Feeling genuinely adored and acknowledged will help your youngster more than anything else.

Try not to surrender. It's difficult to foresee the course of mental imbalance range jumble. Try not to rush to make judgment calls about the thing life will resemble for your kid. Like every other person, individuals with mental imbalances have a whole lifetime to develop and foster their capacities.

Assisting your youngster with mental imbalance flourish tip 1: Give construction and wellbeing
Realizing all you can about chemical imbalance and engaging in treatment will go far toward aiding your kid. Moreover, the accompanying tips will make everyday home life simpler for both you and your kid with ASD:

Be reliable. Kids with ASD struggle with applying what they've realized in one setting (like the specialist's office or school) to other people, including the home. For instance, your youngster might utilize communication via gestures at school to impart, however never remember to do as such at home. Establishing consistency in your youngster's current circumstance is the most effective way to build up learning. Figure out what your youngster's specialists are doing and proceed with their methods at home. Investigate the chance of having treatment occur in more than one spot to urge your kid to move what the person has gained starting with one climate and then onto the next. It's likewise essential to be predictable in the manner you collaborate with your kid and manage testing ways of behaving.

Adhere to a timetable. Medically introverted youngsters will generally be best when they have an exceptionally organized timetable or schedule. Once more, this returns to the consistency the two of them need and long for. Set up a timetable for your youngster, with customary times for feasts, treatment, school, and sleep time. Attempt to downplay interruptions. Assuming there is an undeniable timetable change, set up your youngster for it ahead of time.

Reward acceptable conduct. Encouraging feedback can go quite far with kids with ASD, so try to "discover them accomplishing something great." Recognition them when they act suitably or get familiar with another ability, being unmistakable about the thing conduct they're being lauded for. Likewise search for alternate ways of remunerating them for a good way of behaving, for example, giving them a sticker or allowing them to play with a most loved toy.

Make a home security zone. Cut out a confidential space in your home where your youngster can unwind, have a solid sense of reassurance, and be protected. This will include sorting out and defining limits in manners your youngster can comprehend. Viewable signals can be useful (hued tape checking untouchable regions, marking things in the house with pictures). You may likewise have to somewhere safe and secure proof the house, especially assuming that your kid is inclined to fits or other self-harmful ways of behaving.

Tip 2: Track down nonverbal ways of interfacing

Associating a mentally unbalanced kid can be testing, yet you don't have to talk — or even touch — to impart and bond. You convey by how you take a gander at your kid, by your manner of speaking, your non-verbal communication - and potentially how you contact your kid. Your kid is likewise speaking with you, regardless of whether the individual in question won't ever talk. You simply have to gain proficiency with the language.

Search for nonverbal signs. Assuming you are perceptive and mindful, you can figure out how to get on the nonverbal prompts that mentally unbalanced kids use to convey. Focus on the sorts of sounds they make, their looks, and the signals they use when they're worn out, hungry, or need something.

Sort out the inspiration driving the fit of rage. It's simply normal to feel upset when you are misconstrued or disregarded, and it's the same for kids with ASD. At the point when youngsters with ASD showcase, it's frequently because you're not getting on their nonverbal signs. Pitching a fit is their approach to imparting their disappointment and standing out enough to be noticed.

Set aside a few minutes for entertainment only. A youngster adapting to ASD is as yet a kid. For both mentally unbalanced kids and their folks, there should be something else to live besides treatment. Plan recess when your kid is generally ready and alert. Sort out ways of having a great time together by pondering the things that make your youngster grin, giggle, and emerge from her/his shell. Your kid is probably going to partake in these exercises most if they don't appear to be restorative or instructive. There are colossal advantages that outcome from your delight in your kid's organization and from your kid's happiness regarding investing unpressured energy with you. Having is a fundamental influence on learning for all youngsters and shouldn't feel like work.

Focus on your youngster's tangible awareness. Numerous youngsters with ASD are easily affected by light, sound, contact, taste, and smell. A few youngsters with mental imbalances are "under-delicate" to tactile boosts. Sort out what sights, sounds, scents, developments, and material sensations trigger your child's "terrible" or troublesome ways of behaving and what gets a positive reaction. What does your youngster view as upsetting? Quieting? Awkward? Charming? Assuming you comprehend what influences your kid, you'll be better at investigating issues, forestalling circumstances that cause hardships, and making effective encounters.

Tip 3: Make a customized mental imbalance treatment plan

With so many various medicines accessible, it very well may be difficult to sort out which approach is appropriate for your kid. Making things more confounded, you might hear unique or in any event, clashing proposals from guardians, educators, and specialists.

While assembling a treatment plan for your youngster, remember that there is no single treatment that works for everybody. Every individual in the chemical imbalance range is exceptional, with various qualities and shortcomings.

Your youngster's treatment ought to be custom fitted as per their singular requirements. You realize your kid best, so it ultimately depends on you to ensure those necessities are being met. You can do that by posing yourself the accompanying inquiries:

What are my kid's assets - and their shortcomings?

What ways of behaving are creating the most issues? What significant abilities is my youngster lacking?

How does my kid learn best - through seeing, tuning in, or doing?

What does my kid appreciate - and how might those exercises be utilized in the treatment and reinforce learning?

At long last, remember that regardless of what treatment plan is picked, your association is fundamental to progress. You can assist your kid with seeking the most out of treatment by working inseparably with the treatment group and finishing the treatment at home. (To this end your prosperity is fundamental!)

A decent treatment plan will:
Expand on your youngster's advantages.
Offer an anticipated timetable.
Show undertakings as a progression of straightforward advances.
Effectively connect with your kid's consideration in profoundly organized exercises.
Give standard support of conduct.
Include the guardians.
Picking mental imbalance medicines
There is a wide range of choices and ways to deal with ASD treatment, including conduct treatment, discourse language treatment, exercise-based recuperation, word-related treatment, and dietary treatment.

While you don't need to restrict your kid to only each treatment, in turn, it's far-fetched that you'll have the option to address everything simultaneously. All things considered, begin by zeroing in on your youngster's most extreme side effects and squeezing needs.

Tip 4: Track down help and backing
Focusing on a youngster with a chemical imbalance can request a great deal of energy and time. There might be days when you feel overpowered, focused, or deterred. Nurturing is ever difficult, and bringing up a kid with exceptional requirements is considerably really testing. To be the best parent you can be, it's fundamental that you deal with yourself.

Try not to attempt to do everything all alone. You don't need to! There are many spots that groups of kids with ASD can go to for exhortation, some assistance, backing, and backing:

Promotions support gatherings - Joining an ASD support bunch is an extraordinary method for meeting different families managing similar difficulties you are. Guardians can share data, get guidance, and rest on one another for everyday reassurance. Simply being around others in a comparable situation and sharing their experience can go far toward lessening the disconnection many guardians feel in the wake of getting a kid's conclusion.

Rest care - Each parent needs a break from time to time. What's more, for guardians adapting to the additional pressure of ASD, this is particularly obvious. In rest care, another guardian takes over for a brief time, offering you a reprieve for a couple of hours, days, or even weeks.

Early mediation administrations (birth through age two)
Babies and little children through the age of two get help through the Early Mediation program. To qualify, your

youngster should initially go through a free evaluation.

Chapter 4

Speech therapy to do at home for your child:

Youth Language instruction Thoughts for ASD

Picking the right language instruction approach for a youngster relies upon a few variables, including the kid's age, formative level, learning style, and individual interest. Numerous youngsters with chemical imbalances are first analyzed in youth. This is a fundamental time for language abilities, and concentrated language instruction can assist with building significant collaborations.

Energize Creature Commotions

In a non-verbal youngster, take a stab at dealing with creature commotions, as opposed to words. Numerous youngsters with chemical imbalances have a partiality toward creatures, and this can fabricate a close-to-home association. Use toy horse shelters, creature trains, or whatever another toy that intrigues the youngster

Brief "More"
"More" is a significant word for utilitarian correspondence and utilizing swinging or another most loved movement is an extraordinary method for empowering the youngster to give this a shot. Swing the youngster briefly and afterward stop the swing and trust that the kid will make the "more" hand sign or give the signal "more."

Set Up Solicitation Circumstances
Place most loved toys or food things barely out of the youngster's compass however well inside view. The youngster should signal or ask somehow or another to get the thing. Urge the youngster to take this to the following correspondence level, for example, going from driving the

grown-up by the hand to verbally mentioning the thing.

Fabricate Conversational Schedules
For some children on the range, routine is vital. Construct conversational schedules to assist with empowering language. For instance, place the youngster at the highest point of the slide, and hold the person in question back from going down. Say, "Prepared, set... " and trust that the youngster will say "Go!" When the kid says "go," reward the person in question with the slide.

Reward Going to Their Name
One of the signs of chemical imbalance in youth is that youngsters on the range may not move in the direction of their names. This will be fundamental correspondence expertise, so reward the kid with a little treat or a most loved movement each time the individual in question turns when you call.

Get on the Floor

With any offspring of this age or formative level, a great deal of playtime occurs on the floor. You can energize collaboration and correspondence by getting down on the kid's level and playing with something very similar.

Demand a Turn

Embed yourself in the drop in the bucket by taking a turn from time to time. For example, if the youngster is playing with a vehicle slope, take the vehicle from the person in question and put it down the incline. Then, at that point, urging the youngster to say "my turn" to get the vehicle back.

Pick a Cherished Turn-Taking Game

Further, energize turn-taking by utilizing a game the youngster particularly appreciates. Numerous youngsters on the range are exceptionally visual, so a game like "Memory" might be number one. Alternating in a game like this will assist the youngster with getting ready for conversational turn-taking.

Work on Remarking on a Common Movement
Practice expressions and methodologies the youngster might use to communicate with peers. This might incorporate remarking on a common movement, like playing with blocks or utilizing the tangible table at school. For instance, reward the youngster for expressing out loud whatever the individual in question is working on while at the same time playing with blocks

Model Imagine Play

Model normal imagine mess around that preschoolers appreciate, utilizing age-suitable language abilities. Models incorporate playing house, playing eatery, playing supermarket, and professing to be a specialist or veterinarian. If the youngster knows all about these schedules and the related language, the person in question will find lasting success with peers.

Practice Shared Consideration Games
Practice imparted consideration abilities to games like "I Spy." To do this, gaze at something self-evident, and have the youngster think about the thing you're checking out. This will assist the youngster with the conversational point of view.

Play a Motion Speculating Game
Non-verbal correspondence can be really difficult for youngsters on the range, so it's great to mess around to rehearse this

expertise. Take a stab at playing a signal game where a youngster is compensated for accurately speculating the significance of a motion. Begin by giving a few models and assisting the youngster with giving the signals a shot. Incorporate pointing, shrugging, gesturing "yes" and "no," crossing arms, stepping feet, and that's only the tip of the iceberg.

Primary School Language instruction Thoughts for ASD

In primary school, things frequently get more requests for youngsters on the range. They might have to arrange convoluted non-verbal social collaborations, and their correspondence distinctions might turn out to be more obvious to peers. Attempt a portion of these methodologies while working with rudimentary matured youngsters.

Instruct Marking Sentiments
Work on marking sentiments. Use animation drawings and stories to assist youngsters with distinguishing how a person is feeling and recommend suitable language-based reactions for that inclination. If the youngster has a most loved book or character, attract this interest to represent this idea.

Energize Inquiry Posing
Train youngsters to seek clarification on some pressing issues. One method for doing this is to conceal a toy or article in a pack and have the youngster ask what it is. Extend this activity by thinking of social inquiries the youngster can pose to a companion.

Work with Social Correspondence
Youngsters on the range frequently need a little assistance utilizing language to communicate with peers. You can work

with at least two kids together to assist with working with social correspondence. It might assist with having them work from content and have them play an organized game. Reward the youngsters with commendation or a little treat.

Put on a Stance Play
Model non-verbal correspondence with the youngster as a play. It's particularly essential to deal with body pose, for example, dismissing or crossing the arms. Work with the youngster to compose content with these communications in it and afterward act it out together.

Benefit from Extraordinary Interests
Numerous youngsters on the range have extraordinary exceptional interests. Utilize these interests for your potential benefit to save the youngster who participated in the collaboration for longer periods. You can chip away at

questions and replies, turn-taking, non-verbal correspondence, and numerous other significant ideas.

Remember About Unstructured Settings

At this age, a few youngsters on the range become great at involving social language in an organized setting like the study hall, however, they battle in unstructured circumstances like the break room or jungle gym. Notice the youngster in these circumstances and take a stab at changing the treatment routine to zero in on the difficulties they present. For example, work on down-to-earth abilities like joining a table in the break room.

Center School and Secondary School Language instruction Thoughts for Chemical imbalance

In center school and secondary school, prevailing difficulties become significantly more extraordinary. You might have to zero in your treatment approach on non-verbal companion collaborations and fundamental abilities the kid should prevail after school. Attempt a portion of these thoughts.

Practice Abilities Locally
Go out into the local area with the youngster, first seeing how the social collaborations happen and afterward having the kid take an interest. For example, have a youngster watch others put in a lunch request at an eatery, then, at that point, discuss how the communication occurred. Climb to having the youngster put in the request.

Work on Capricious Circumstances
Work on answering capricious individuals and collaborations. It very well may be upsetting when somebody acts out of the blue. Discuss methodologies, for example, undivided attention or marking sentiments, that the

youngster can use to arrange these circumstances.

Work on Dating Behavior

Dating manners and inverse orientation communications can be trying for youngsters on the range. As they progress in years, it's essential to chip away at the language abilities required for these collaborations. Practice these communications with content, including asking somebody for a date, eating at an eatery, and meeting somebody's folks.

Have a Counterfeit Prospective employee meeting

Practice prospective employee meeting abilities with the youngster. Many children have part-time or summer occupations during secondary school, and these abilities will prove to be useful. Have a gathering of children put on a counterfeit prospective employee meeting where they should pose inquiries of each other and introduce themselves expertly.

Show Compromise

Compromise can be trying for a youngster on the range. Utilize visual guides and practice collaborations to assist the youngster with separating the communication and take part in a useful and self-assured manner. Compose a content together of a run-of-the-mill struggle and the choices for settling it, like undivided attention or enjoying some time off to chill off.

Chapter 5

How to teach self care for your child

Taking care of oneself has never been a one-size-fits-all peculiarity, yet for guardians with youngsters on the range seldom really does any measure appear to fit. Tracking down sitters, going on getaways, and the wide range of various usually suggested taking care of oneself exercises are frequently tormented with obstructions and bands to go through if you have a kid with a chemical imbalance.

In any case, guardians who immerse their neurodiverse kids need and have the right to track down techniques for taking care of themselves that work, so they can top themselves off as well. In any case, they're not helping themselves or their youngsters.

Taking care of oneself will appear to be unique for everybody; it's not about bubble showers. It may very well be picking things that can make your life somewhat simpler. Here is some reasonable and interesting taking care of oneself ideas for guardians of medically introverted kids, some of which I've done myself.

Permit Yourself to Have Needs
"As guardians of medically introverted youngsters, we want outside exercises that don't have anything to do with a mental imbalance,"

says Keisha Pruden, authorized specialist, and proprietor of Pruden Guiding Ideas. "Indeed, I realize that can appear to be unimaginable, yet if we can be imaginative with our kids' necessities, we can be innovative with our own as well," she makes sense of.

For some guardians, bringing up youngsters implies surrendering portions of yourself, like your spare energy, side interests, and a decent night's rest in addition to other things. Nonetheless, a major piece of taking care of oneself while nurturing neurodivergent kids is keeping a personality beyond them and doing it in any case you see fit.

I needed to relearn what it intended to put myself first and recognize my cravings. While it very well might be too difficult to even think about thinking about any side interests you could practically take up, it's not difficult to recognize your needs of the day essentially. Indeed, even something as straightforward as partaking in some homegrown tea while it's warm could be a beginning in easing pressure and rehearsing taking care of oneself.

"Empowering guardians to reserve margin for themselves is a strong signal that likewise advises them that they're worth the effort," says Tasha Holland-Kornegay, Ph.D., wellbeing master for Nike and proprietor of Our Treatment Place.

Request Help
Great sitters can be rare, and it very well may be significantly more troublesome and exorbitant to find somebody who can convey the particular consideration neurodiverse youngsters require. Thus, guardians wind up wearing themselves out by doing everything all alone.

Life as a parent for youngsters with chemical imbalance implies requesting help as well as tolerating it too. Relief care can be very useful in getting quality providing care administrations on the off chance that you want a break. Or on the other hand, in any event, tolerating solace food from associations, for example, Lasagna Love or a feast train can be useful in giving yourself relief from preparing and dinner arranging so you can rehearse taking care of yourself.

Exploit Freebees and Advantages
While examining chemical imbalance you're probably going to find out about the dissatisfactions and snags that you'll have to survive. Be that as it may, you seldom find out about the benefits. A portion of those benefits incorporate the capacity to get an impairment bulletin/tag in certain states, passes to skip lines at entertainment meccas, or even government-managed retirement relying upon your pay. On the off chance that you don't know whether it's feasible to get extraordinary access or facilities, inquire. On the off chance that it will make your everyday existence more

straightforward, it merits asking and having.

Deal with Your Psychological well-being From ABA treatment to language training, to mental social treatment and that's only the tip of the iceberg, you probably invest a fair measure of energy pursuing, guiding your kid to, and partaking in different treatments to help your kid. In any case, it is vital to focus on treatment for yourself.

"It's certainly useful to get mental imbalance explicit treatment to learn to conduct the board systems and gain psychoeducation around what guardians can anticipate from their neurodiverse kid," says Hayley Wilds, authorized instructor and proprietor of Community for Imaginative Directing.

Be that as it may, taking part in family treatment can be a magnificent taking care of oneself methodology notwithstanding chemical imbalance explicit administrations. Family treatment can assist the family in fostering a family with organizing that upholds the extraordinary difficulties that accompany mental imbalance. It can likewise permit reality for guardians to lament or adjust their assumptions and expectations for their kid, work to acknowledge their youngster's neurodiversity and all that accompanies it, and foster another casing that praises their kid and family personality, she makes sense of.

Track down an Emotionally supportive network
On the off chance that a specialist is far off, support gatherings can be so useful in filling in the holes of getting conclusions, tips, and discovering a true sense of harmony.

"[You need] a group of friends that gets it," says Pruden. "Having a little gathering of loved ones who comprehend my life might be occupied in light of mental imbalance related exercises has been so significant in my profound life."

Indeed, even gatherings via online entertainment like Dark Mental imbalance Mothers (B.A.M.), Mental imbalance Guardians Care Group, and meetings such as Mental imbalance in Dark and Public Chemical imbalance Gathering can offer local area and backing.

Pick Your Fights
At the point when you wind up battling everybody from your protection supplier, to your parents-in-law about whether your kid even has a chemical imbalance, and educators for not following the IEP, consistently can feel like conflict.

While certain battles might be around for some time, there might be some you'll find simply do not merit the battle. Perhaps declining to make sense of mental imbalance for a colleague isn't in any event, attempting to comprehend. Perhaps it's stopping contentions with your youngster to trim their hair amid their tactile issues and simply allowing it to develop out. Anything it is, inquire as to whether it merits the battle and if perhaps venturing back will bring a little simplicity back into your life.

Search for Your Kid's Assets

Since a chemical imbalance finding frequently requires a greater number of treatments and medical checkups than a commonly created kid, it likewise implies investing more energy examining everything "wrong" with your kid. It's a good idea that guardians feel overpowered, miserable, and disappointed while zeroing in on negatives so much of the time.

It additionally may not be smart for the youngster. Invest energy thinking about your kid's assets and discuss those as well. Talking about all the decency that came from the conclusion could do ponders in the taking care of oneself division.

Give Yourself Elegance

At last, a huge yet essential piece of taking care of oneself while nurturing youngsters with mental imbalance is giving yourself effortlessness. It's not difficult to feel the parental disgrace of reasoning you're not doing what's necessary. There can be such a lot of you don't have any idea, feel like you passed up, or fault yourself for that you wind up feeling remorseful, disappointed, and worn out. Nonetheless, bringing down your assumptions in certain circumstances, excusing yourself, and celebrating even the little wins can go quite far in self-safeguarding.

Believe that you are doing all that can be expected with your conditions. At the point when you lift yourself, your capacity to deal with yourself and your kid improves, specialists recommend.

Permitting yourself to feel anything that you want to feel can help, says Holland-Kornegay. Cutting out space to self-reflect is at the core of tending to the feeling of "being lost,", particularly for guardians of youngsters with a chemical imbalance.

"Such a large number of my clients depended on evasion to keep an eye on their inner states as though they ought to help everyone around them however never themselves," she said. "It's a stage toward finding out about yourself corresponding to the world and the chemical imbalance local area, and grasping your inclination about your job as a parent and your future."

There's no correct method for interfacing with these encounters - as long as you practice self-esteem and attempt to comprehend your sentiments, you're on the correct way.

Chapter 6

How to help your child make friends:

As a parent it is typical to stress over your kid's turn of events and whether they are advancing toward cheerful and practical adulthood. Assuming your kid is in the chemical imbalance range, you realize that he might have a couple of additional obstacles to moving beyond different kids.

Perhaps the greatest trouble confronting youngsters with ASD is social collaboration. Creating companions can be somewhat terrifying for any youngster, however, for the kid with ASD, it tends to dismay. Here are a few hints to help make companions somewhat simpler to explore.

Conversing with Different Children About Mental imbalance

Kids frequently perceive things they don't have the language to make sense of. Your kid's cohorts have likely currently understood that your youngster is fairly unique concerning them. A few guardians conclude that sharing data about their youngster's exceptional requirements with peers and their folks is a useful method for building understanding and fellowships.

This decision isn't a great fit for everybody, except if you choose to share data about your kid's extra learning and social necessities with different children, adopting a considered and cooperative strategy is significant.

You might wish to look for the exhortation of a specialist in the field, for example, the school's advisor, learning support educator, or outside clinician to work with you to plan. Including the homeroom, the instructor is likewise imperative since the individual will be the individual who needs to manage inquiries from different understudies (and perhaps their folks) after your youngster's determination is revealed.

While visiting the class to discuss what chemical imbalance and what makes your kid one of a kind isn't a great fit for everybody, many guardians have decided to do this report that loads of children take the data in their steps. Other kids' ability for sympathy might shock you, and in this day of advanced media, where data about mental imbalance is all the more unreservedly accessible, you may likewise observe that their folks are understanding and strong as well.

Assist Your Youngster With distinguishing Who A Companion Is
It might sound straightforward, yet your kid may not perceive it regardless of whether somebody is their companion. The 'pseudo-nemesis' is perfectly healthy in many schools, and children who act in this way will frequently profess to be your

youngster's companion, however at that point say or do pernicious things that may be entertaining for them, yet confounding and disturbing for your kid.

If you imagine that your kid's kindness is being exploited along these lines, take a stab at asking them inquiries like, "Would you like to invest energy with somebody who calls you mean names?" Or, "What do you appreciate about investing time with Jenny?" Attempt to stay away from unique ideas like, "A companion is somebody who acknowledges you." As the parent of a kid with a chemical imbalance, you realize that he thinks in strict terms. You should, hence, give him substantial models like, "A companion is somebody who imparts their things to you, who is great and asks what games you might want to play."

What's more, let your kid's educator in on that you suspect something is out of order in the jungle gym. This will offer the school the chance to screen the kids' all's cooperation and to guarantee that your youngster is protected.

Practice, Practice, Practice
It is not difficult to feel overpowered or mistaken for a circumstance on the off chance that you feel ill-equipped. For bunches of children determined to have a mental imbalance, pretends are an extraordinary method for rehearsing the flightiness of jungle gym discussions.

Take a stab at rehearsing the inquiries that your youngster could pose to start a discussion. Likewise, examine with him proper reactions to normal social collaborations. For instance, you could show him how to answer on the off chance that somebody acquaints themselves or offers to shake hands. You could show him suitable ways of starting communication. You could likewise compose scripts together of how discussions can advance so that when defied with another circumstance, he can answer with certainty.

If your youngster is exceptionally visual, drawing these speculative discussions as an animation strip could be a method for assisting him with pondering what he would agree that in light of others.

Extracurricular Exercises: The method for meeting similar mates
It's not generally simple to meet similar mates in the jungle gym, however, beyond school, numerous exercises could arouse your youngster's curiosity and proposition social open doors.

What is your kid inspired by? On the off chance that he cherishes transport, a nearby model train club may be only the road he wants to meet different fans. Does she cherish science and innovation?

Look out for mechanical technology, coding, Lego, or configuration projects, for example, Tinker Tank or Blocks for Youngsters. Exercises like Fledglings and Scouts are additionally frequently perfect for 'advanced' youngsters with chemical imbalance since they are interest-based and ordinarily have a seriously high proportion of grown-up to kid support.

Offering your kid chances to meet with different children who have a typical interest can be a brilliant beginning stage for discussions and associations with the same mature peers.

Plan Play Dates
For youngsters in the mental imbalance range, enormous gatherings of children can plague them. One of the most outstanding ways of producing fellowships is to begin little, with short playdates with only another kid. However, if you will sort out a playdate,

there are a couple of things you want to be aware of.

Kids who battle to make social associations frequently need construction to assist them with dealing with the social nervousness they feel, so have a couple of exercises arranged when your youngster welcomes a companion to your home. Remember to have a bite arranged, as well. It is something else that treats can make everything go smoothly in social connections.

Timing and span of playdates are vital to their prosperity. Ensure that first gatherings are quick and painless, long enough to have a great time, yet not insofar as to break anybody down.

At first, you might need to remain nearby and direct your kid as he wants it. As the fellowship advances and the kids become more alright with each other, you can drift less.

Additionally, don't become too worried about the kids connecting the entire time. Assuming they take part in an equal play, that is fine since even commonly creating youngsters participate in an equal play. The primary target of a playdate is for everybody to live it up.

Making a companion takes time
Your medically introverted kid might have more trouble managing social connections than the commonplace kid, yet with consolation and backing from you, it is feasible to assemble your kid's certainty and assist him with exploring the social scene.

The main thing isn't to surrender!

Kids who are 'on the range' can and do make companions yet some of the time it requires a little investment to track down the right associations. Remain confident, be patient, and continue to search for conditions in which your youngster will track down similar companions.

Your kid's giggling and grins when he, at last, observes that companion merits the stand-by!

Chapter 7

How to teach your child how to be social:

Home/Family Guide/5 Methods for working on Interactive abilities for Medically introverted Youngsters
5 Methods for working on Interactive abilities for Medically introverted Kids

Mental imbalance's Effect on Interactive abilities
Chemical imbalance is a formative problem that can influence how an individual conveys, communicates with their general surroundings, and deals with feelings.

Interactive abilities are framed through customary collaborations with individuals. Since kids with mental imbalance struggle with understanding and understanding others, interactive abilities frequently should be instructed unexpectedly.

The CDC distributes that side effects of mental imbalance connected with interactive abilities and collaborations include:

Powerlessness to "read" others.
Hardships with to and fro discussions and associations.
Poor nonverbal relational abilities and ways of behaving, and trouble grasping these signals in others.
Inconvenience changes ways of behaving to the circumstance, frequently bringing about unseemly ways of behaving.
Indifference for peers.
No craving for fanciful or cooperative play.
Resoluteness with schedules and timetables.
Tactile awarenesses.
Trouble answering social communications or starting them.

Chemical imbalance is a range problem, and that implies it can have shifting levels of seriousness and incapacity.

A few youngsters are advanced. They can veil mental imbalance side effects until prevalent difficulties fabricate and turn out to be excessively tremendous for them. This frequently concurs with entering a profoundly friendly climate like school.

Others with chemical imbalance relapse in language and coordinated abilities. Formative postponements are apparent as soon as a half year old, however, they may not present until some other time in toddlerhood. Chemical imbalance can be analyzed as soon as a year and a half, however, it is most frequently analyzed around age 3.

Interactive abilities can be restricted or different in a kid with chemical imbalance no matter what the seriousness of the problem. By and large, a more significant level of inability implies a more critical effect on conduct, relational abilities, and social connections.

The most effective method to Lift Interactive abilities in Mentally unbalanced Youngsters
Assuming that your kid has restricted interactive abilities, it doesn't mean they are bound to experience this way until the end of their life.

Mentally unbalanced youngsters can benefit significantly from treatment, especially applied conduct examination (ABA) treatment, which is viewed as the best treatment for chemical imbalance. If a kid's interactive abilities are additionally restricted by correspondence issues, for example, discourse issues, language training may likewise be suggested.

Guardians are vital to a kid's prosperity. With cognizant endeavors to execute the examples learned in treatment consistently and uplifting feedback, guardians can assist their youngsters with bettering speaking with their general surroundings.

Generally, mentally unbalanced youngsters can see significant enhancements in their interactive abilities because of treatment and parental work at home.

The following are five methods for working on your kid's interactive abilities:

1. Build up Certain Ways of behaving and Observe Qualities

Uplifting feedback has for quite some time been a technique to remunerate great ways of behaving in a non punitive manner to support them. This can be particularly successful for mentally unbalanced youngsters.

Frequently, mentally unbalanced youngsters probably won't comprehend what is generally anticipated of them and why. By offering acclaim and support for prosocial ways of behaving, guardians, and educators can assist with shaping the way of behaving and developing wanted interactive abilities.

To build up certain ways of behaving and interactive abilities:

Track down a reinforcer that works. It very well may be consumable, visual, substantial, verbal, an action, or social consideration.

Convey the support at the earliest opportunity after the ideal way of behaving — in 5 seconds is ideal.

Fluctuate the reinforcers. This can keep things intriguing and keep the youngster connected longer.

Change out reinforcers depending on the situation. On the off chance that one support procedure or reinforcer isn't filling in as well as it has previously, thinks about changing everything around.

Gradually back down on utilizing reinforcers after you have made progress with a specific way of behaving. After some time, you need to reach a place where the way of behaving is set, and you never again need to support it.

Show restraint. Positive conduct changes don't happen all of a sudden. They take time, exertion, and practice.

To additional upgrade interactive abilities, exploit the kid's assets. Medically introverted kids frequently have a specific area of interest or skill. Featuring this in a group environment can assist mentally unbalanced kids with figuring out how to socially interface. Since they feel happier with discussing this area of interest, it can remove a portion of the underlying clumsiness of the social connection.

2. Model and Practice Wanted Ways of behaving
All kids learn ways of behaving by watching. They frequently see a way of behaving and mirror it. Guardians can show kids how to act in friendly circumstances by showing them how.

With mentally unbalanced kids, guardians will normally have to make this a stride further. Medically introverted youngsters frequently fail to see what they are seeing, so they need assistance deciphering the way of behaving. If guardians separate the social cooperation and clarify it for them, mentally unbalanced youngsters can get a superior handle on mastering these abilities.

Pretending can be an extraordinary method for assisting medically introverted kids with rehearsing interactive abilities and collaborations. Guardians can plan what is happening and afterward stroll through it with the kid early on to assist them with understanding what's in store and how to properly mingle.

Pretending can likewise offer your kid the opportunity to try and learn in an okay circumstance. You are not too far off to give ideas and remedies depending on the situation without the pressure of a public climate.

While pretending, alternate. If you are pretending to have a specific shared communication, it tends to be helpful for the mentally unbalanced kid to assume the part of their friend. This can assist them with acquiring a superior comprehension of others and communication overall. You should talk them through how their friend might be feeling in this present circumstance.

Messing around together at home can assist medically introverted kids with figuring out how to alternate, keep the guidelines, and be a decent game. While playing the game, notice your kid's way of behaving and talk them through what's in store and what is generally anticipated of them.

Instances of straightforward games that can assist with interactive abilities include:

Passing a ball this way and that.
Simon Says.

Basic card and tabletop games.
Find the stowaway.

3. Give Organized Social Associations

Youngsters with chemical imbalance value construction and soundness. Change can be troublesome. Schedules are significant.

Thus, it very well may be more straightforward to show new abilities and improve interactive abilities while working inside a normal construction. Guardians can set up little, organized social corporations to deal with interactive abilities before youngsters need to convey these abilities into a bigger setting, like a homeroom.

During these organized corporations, spread out the assumptions direct, so everybody understands what ways of behaving are expected and expected of them. Abilities can be educated early on at home and afterward converted into little social scenes with a couple of friends at first.

These elevated degrees of design in early corporations can urge a mentally unbalanced kid to be more adaptable. They figure out how to connect and develop inside the set boundaries, and they feel better in their activities. This continuously permits them to be more adaptable in circumstances with less design.

4. Talk Through Conceivable Social Situations and Utilize Visual Guides
Preparing a medically introverted kid for social circumstances is critical. These discussions assist your kid with finding out about their general surroundings and constructing the apparatuses to associate well in friendly circumstances.

Converse with your kid about likely friendly circumstances and occasions, and how to fittingly answer. It is useful to offer a visual portrayal, for example,

Pictures
Drawings
Recordings
A visual portrayal of friend communications can assist mentally unbalanced youngsters with realizing what's in store and give them extra assets to display. Express what's going on in these scenes to build up acknowledged interactive abilities and anticipated ways of behaving.

Social instructing is a type of discussion and visual portrayal that includes assisting the kid with figuring out how to turn out to be more mindful of their particular activities and expert the social difficulties that mental imbalance presents. Social instruction can incorporate recording cooperations and stroll through them with the kid later. As you watch the recordings, distinguish specific ways of behaving and offer input.

5. Set the Climate for Progress
Mentally unbalanced youngsters blossom with construction and schedule. They frequently have tactile issues, like aversion to noisy commotions or splendid lights.

Consider both these focuses while working with your youngster on friendly associations. During showing minutes, downplay outside interruptions. Pick times when your kid is generally loose and adept to need to work with you.

Keep room lights darkened and limit commotions to advance learning. Ensure your kid isn't eager or excessively drained while attempting to show a genuinely new thing. Social correspondence is best when presented in an open setting.

Center around just showing the particular interactive ability. It tends to be hard for a mentally unbalanced kid to ingest a social illustration on the off chance that they are centered around something different too.

Enhancements Take Time
Mentally unbalanced kids can encounter huge additions in interactive abilities, however, they don't occur right away. Be predictable with treatment and the illustrations you support at home. Over the long haul, you'll see improvement.